GW00373891

# Piano
# Grade 4

## Pieces & Exercises
for Trinity Guildhall examinations

## 2012-2014

Published by
Trinity College London
Registered Office:
89 Albert Embankment
London SE1 7TP UK

T +44 (0)20 7820 6100
F +44 (0)20 7820 6161
E music@trinityguildhall.co.uk
www.trinityguildhall.co.uk

Registered in the UK
Company no. 02683033
Charity no. 1014792

Copyright © 2011 Trinity College London

**Unauthorised photocopying is illegal**
No part of this publication may be copied or reproduced in any
form or by any means without the prior permission of the publisher.

Printed in England by Halstan & Co. Ltd, Amersham, Bucks.

# Allemande in A minor

## HWV 478

George Frideric Handel
(1685-1759)

Dynamics are editorial. Chords may be arpeggiated on the beat.

Copyright © 2011 Trinity College London

3

# Rondo
## 2nd movement from Sonatina in F, Anh 5

Ludwig van Beethoven
(1770-1827)

Dynamics and articulation in square brackets are editorial.

Copyright © 2011 Trinity College London

( 2 )

( 3 ) Players with small hands may omit the bracketed notes.

# Allegretto

### from Sonatina in G, op. 55 no. 2

Friedrich Kuhlau
(1786-1832)

( *1* ) Players with small hands may omit the bracketed notes.

Copyright © 2011 Trinity College London

# Kaki-no-Tane

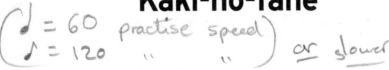

Akira Yuyama
(born 1932)

Composer's metronome mark ♩ = c. **152**.

Copyright © Zen-On Music Company Ltd. Reprinted by permission.

# Solfeggio in F

### K. 393 (385b) no. 2

Wolfgang Amadeus Mozart
(1756-1791)

Dynamics are editorial.

Copyright © 2011 Trinity College London

# Sicilienne

## no. 11 from *Album for the Young* op. 68

Robert Schumann
(1810–1856)

Copyright © 2011 Trinity College London

# A Sad Story

no. 6 from *Thirty Pieces for Children* op. 27

Dmitri Kabalevsky
(1904–1987)

Copyright © 1938 by Boosey & Hawkes Music Publishers Ltd.
Reproduced by permission of Boosey & Hawkes Music Publishers Ltd.

[Blank page to facilitate page turns]

# Tapping Heels

Alan Bullard
(born 1947)

Composer's metronome mark ♩ = c. **84.**

Copyright © 2006 Spartan Press Music Publishers Limited, Strathmashie House, Laggan, PH20 1BU.
Used by kind permission of the publishers.

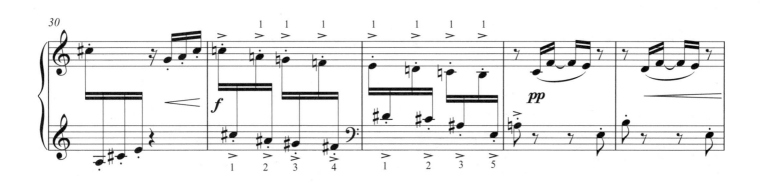

# Never Too Late

Heather Hammond

Composer's metronome mark ♩. = **50**.

Copyright © 2003 Kevin Mayhew Ltd.
Reproduced by permission. Licence Nr. 115040/1.

# Exercises

## 1a. Fun and Games – tone, balance and voicing

## 1b. Solemn Melody – tone, balance and voicing

Copyright © 2011 Trinity College London

## 2a. Floating High, Sinking Low – co-ordination

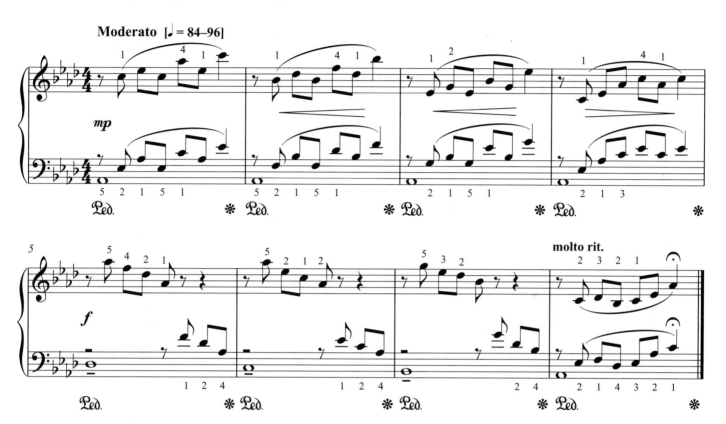

## 2b. Scuttlebugs – co-ordination

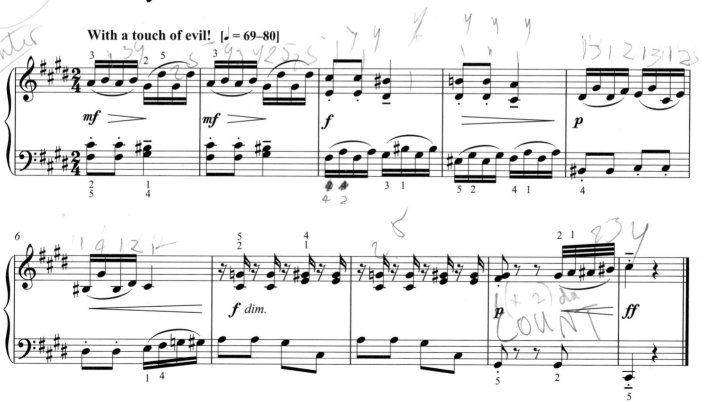

Copyright © 2011 Trinity College London

### 3a. Open Spaces – finger & wrist strength and flexibility

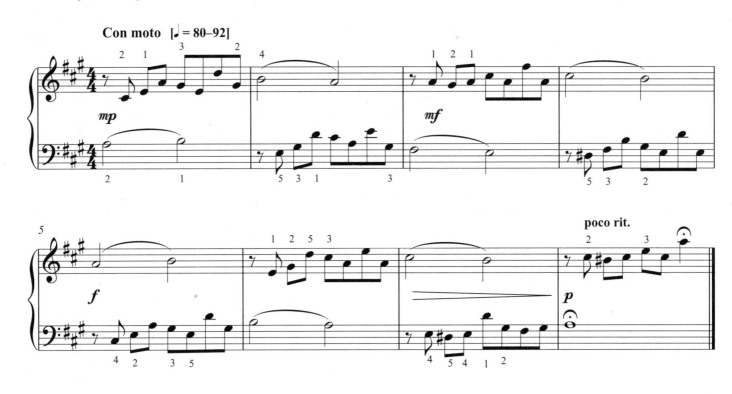

### 3b. Moving In Closer – finger & wrist strength and flexibility

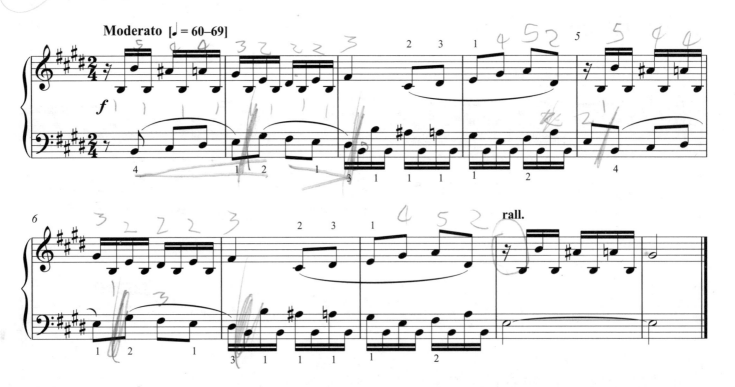

Copyright © 2011 Trinity College London

# Keys / triads

1st Tonic chord (triad)
2nd Supertonic
3rd Mediant
4th Sub dominant
5th dominant
6th sub mediant
7th leading note
8th tonic